Music
& Musicians

ART TODAY!

Acting: Stage & Screen

Art Festivals & Galleries:
The Art of Selling Art

Comedy & Comedians

Filmmaking & Documentaries

Music & Musicians

Painting

Performing Arts

Photography

Sculpting

Writing: Stories, Poetry, Song, & Rap

Music
& Musicians

Z.B. Hill

Mason Crest

Mason Crest
450 Parkway Drive, Suite D
Broomall, PA 19008
www.masoncrest.com

Printed and bound in the United States of America.

First printing
9 8 7 6 5 4 3 2 1

Series ISBN: 978-1-4222-3167-8
ISBN: 978-1-4222-3172-2
ebook ISBN: 978-1-4222-8709-5

Library of Congress Cataloging-in-Publication Data

Hill, Z. B.
  Music & musicians / Z.B. Hill.
    pages cm — (Art today!)
  Includes index.
  ISBN 978-1-4222-3172-2 (hardback) — ISBN 978-1-4222-3167-8 (series) — ISBN 978-1-4222-8709-5 (ebook) 1. Music—History and criticism—Juvenile literature. 2. Music—Vocational guidance—Juvenile literature. I. Title. II. Title: Music and musicians.
  ML3928.H45 2014
  780—dc23
                                                    2014014806

Contents

KEY ICONS TO LOOK FOR:

 Text-Dependent Questions: These questions send the reader back to the text for more careful attention to the evidence presented there.

 Words to Understand: These words with their easy-to-understand definitions will increase the reader's understanding of the text, while building vocabulary skills.

 Series Glossary of Key Terms: This back-of-the book glossary contains terminology used throughout this series. Words found here increase the reader's ability to read and comprehend higher-level books and articles in this field.

 Research Projects: Readers are pointed toward areas of further inquiry connected to each chapter. Suggestions are provided for projects that encourage deeper research and analysis.

 Sidebars: This boxed material within the main text allows readers to build knowledge, gain insights, explore possibilities, and broaden their perspectives by weaving together additional information to provide realistic and holistic perspectives.

Words to Understand

culture: All the art, values, and thoughts that a group of people have in common.

cantata: A medium-length piece of music, often sung by a choir with instrumental accompaniment.

symphonies: Elaborate musical pieces for a full orchestra.

depression: A psychiatric disorder where someone feels hopeless and sad for a long period of time.

blues: A genre of music based in black American folk culture, often expressing sadness.

classics: Works of art universally recognized to be good or significant.

R&B: Short for Rhythm and Blues, a style of music that started in black American culture in the 1940s.

icon: A person who becomes a symbol of something.

Chapter One

Creating Music

When you think of music, you probably think of it as an art form that's based on sound. Musicians, however, say that music is as much about silence as it is sound. Music creates patterns of sound and silence that please us in some way when we hear them. They make us feel something.

But that doesn't mean that every human being in the world will respond in the same way to the same patterns. There are many kinds of music. Although music has been a part of human life for thousands of years, it has changed down through the eras of history. It was different in different places around the world, with each *culture* developing its own kind of music.

Rhythm and percussion are huge parts of music. Bobbing your head to a beat or tapping your toe is a part of being human.

THE ELEMENTS OF MUSIC

When we talk about music being patterns of sound and silence, we can break down those patterns into several elements. These are pitch, rhythm, melody, harmony, texture, and timbre. All these elements work together to produce the emotional responses we have to music.

Our ears pick up sound waves and our brains interpret them. Pitch depends on the frequency of these waves—how close together the waves are. Our minds perceive sound waves that come more closely together as being "high," while sound waves that move more slowly sound "low."

Make Connections: What Is Art?

It's hard to define exactly what art is. A lot of the time, when we use the word, we're thinking of the visual arts, the ones we can see, like paintings and sculptures. But there are also performing arts, like theater and dance. Music is a performing art, but in today's world, music can also be recorded, which means it can be saved and appreciated for years to come, the way a painting or a sculpture can be. People who try to define what all these different kinds of art have in common say that all art is creative (it expresses the human imagination, our ability to make something new) and communicates emotion in some way. It may also make us think about something important. It is usually considered to be beautiful—although we each may define beauty differently. When it comes to music, what one person loves may sound like only noise to another person!

This is what we call "pitch." We notice pitch in people's voices, as well as in music. The musical scale—do, re, mi, fa, so, la, ti, do, for example—is a way to express pitch in a written form.

Rhythm has to do with patterns of both silence and sound. The world is full of rhythm—the tap-tap of footsteps, the patter of rainfall, the beat and sigh of traffic in the street, the tick-tock of an old-fashioned clock, and—most basic of all to human life—the thump-thump-thump of our hearts. Some scientists believe that the pulse of the human heart is what makes us respond to rhythm so strongly; this pattern of beats has been a part of us since we first began to exist. Our hearts beat more loudly and quickly when we are excited, more slowly and quietly when we are calm, and we respond to musical rhythm in much the same way: music that has a fast, loud beat stirs us up and excites us, while we may feel soothed and peaceful when we hear music with a gentle, slow beat. "Tempo" is the word we use to talk about how fast or slow the beats come in a piece of music.

When we combine pitch and rhythm in a specific way, we get a melody. A melody is a group of tones coming one after another in a specific way. They form a pattern our brains can recognize. Now we're no longer hearing single notes; they've combined into something new that we can repeat. It may even get stuck in our heads, so that we find ourselves humming it over and over.

A melody can be very simple. Harmony adds to that simple line of pitch and rhythm. It makes a piece of music more complex, by throwing in other pitches and rhythms at the same time that the melody's line is moving along. It makes the music more interesting. Some kinds of music depend more on harmony than others, and there are different kinds of harmony. Some harmonies blend into the melody and support it, while others call our attention to the musical spaces outside the melody.

Music that has lots of layers of harmonies is sometimes described as having a thicker "texture." A thick texture could also be produced by having many instruments produce a piece of music—strings, brass, and wind, for example—or many voices, all singing different parts, from soprano (high voices) through bass (low voices).

Timbre is maybe the hardest musical element to define. It's the "quality of a musical note," the mysterious thing that makes us hear a note produced by a human voice as different from the very same note produced by a piano key—and that note in turn as different from the same note produced by a guitar or a trumpet. Even though the note has the very same pitch and loudness, we can still tell the difference. Sometimes musicians also call this "tone quality."

The way that these elements are combined is what makes all the different kinds of music in the world, from classical to rock'n'roll. These elements are what musicians work with, similar to the way that a different kind of artist might work with paint and composition.

TYPES OF MUSICIANS

Just as there are different types of music, there are also different kinds of musicians—people who make music. Some people are very good at performing a specific kind of music; they may use their voices or their instruments to produce music. They may do this alone—or in a group, such as a choir, a band, or an orchestra. Many musicians perform music for purely for their own pleasure (as well as the pleasure of their friends and family). Others, however, get paid for their skills. Professional musicians (musicians who are paid to produce music) might make music for their churches or synagogues; they might give concerts that people pay to attend; they might have jobs where they play instruments in an orchestra; and they might also perform for film production companies, with their music ending up as background for a movie.

Composers and songwriters are special kinds of musicians. They create new pieces of music, rather than performing music that someone else wrote. They combine all the elements of music in a new way, and then write that down so that others can perform it. They may do this for their own pleasure, but they may also get paid for their creative work. Down through the centuries, many great musicians have created new musical works that people continue to enjoy.

FAMOUS MUSICIANS

Johann Sebastian Bach

Bach is often regarded as the greatest composer of all time. Born in 1685 in Germany, he was the youngest of eight children who were born to musical parents. As a child, he sang and played the organ and the violin. When he was ten, both his parents died, but his older brother took him in and continued his musical training. At the age of fifteen, Bach got his first job as a musician; he sang in a school choir. Throughout the rest

Music is an important part of world. It is often especially important to adolescents in the years when they are shaping their own unique identities.

of his life, he would hold many musical posts at schools, churches, and finally in the royal court.

Part of his responsibilities in court was composing new musical pieces. He created hundreds of these, with some of the most famous being the Brandenburg Concertos and *The St. Matthew Passion*. Bach was serious about his faith, and many of his works were intended to be performed in churches. His final job was as an organist and teacher at St. Thomas' Church in Leipzig, where he was also required to create a new *cantata* every week for the Sunday service.

Toward the end of Bach's life, his eyesight began to fail, until he was eventually completely blind. He continued to compose music, however,

In his own day, Bach was best known as an organ player. He left a timeless legacy to the world of music, however.

until he died in 1750. His music is still performed and listened to today, and he is considered to be one of the greatest masters of harmony.

Wolfgang Amadeus Mozart

Mozart is another German musician; he was born in 1756, shortly after Bach died. Mozart was a musical genius. By the time he was four years old, he could learn a piece of music in half an hour. At five, he was playing the clavier (a kind of early piano) with amazing skill, and at six, he began composing his own music; he wrote his first *symphonies* at the age of eight. Mozart traveled all over Europe with his father, who was

Mozart's musical genius was evident from the time he was a young boy. He would grow up to be something of a rebel, and despite his talent, he often offended people by refusing to follow the rules of his day.

a court musician. As they traveled, Mozart's father showed off his son's talents, while the young Mozart had the opportunity to learn from many different kinds of music.

When he got older, he too got jobs at court, where he composed music in every genre of his day. Although he was a brilliant musician, he didn't know how to manage money. He had a reputation for acting silly in the middle of very formal affairs, and he offended many important people. One of his last works, *The Magic Flute*, was so successful, though, that he and his family could finally become financially comfortable—but he died soon after, at the age of thirty-six, from kidney disease. His work has continued to influence the music world ever since, and he is still considered one of the greatest musical geniuses to have ever lived.

Beethoven went deaf, lost his temper, and suffered bouts of terrible depression—and yet he gave the world a great gift of music.

Ludwig van Beethoven

Yet another German composer, Beethoven was born in 1770. Like Mozart, his talent was obvious even when he was a child. His father was also a musician, and he insisted that his son practice the piano playing daily. Beethoven began performing in public when he was seven years old, and he started composing his own work when he was thirteen.

Like many other musicians of his time, when he grew up he was supported by the German royalty. He composed many, many works, but when he was twenty-six, he began to lose his hearing. By the time he died in 1827, he was totally deaf. During these later years of his life, he

This memorial to Robert Johnson in Clarksdale, Mississippi, marks the place where, according to legend, he sold his soul to the devil in exchange for his incredible mastery of the blues.

could no longer perform music, but he never stopped composing it. In fact, some of his greatest works were created after he went deaf, including his Ninth Symphony.

During his lifetime, Beethoven dealt with many challenges, including his deafness, as well as bouts of extreme *depression* and anger at the world. Nevertheless, today he is still considered to be a musical revolutionary who created entire new ways of looking at music. Since Beethoven, many musicians have followed his example; instead of being merely masters of the music that already exists, they have tried to find and create new forms of music.

Robert Johnson

One of these revolutionary musicians was Robert Johnson, who was born centuries after Ludwig Beethoven and created very different music. Johnson was born in 1911 in Mississippi, a dirt-poor black American who grew up to sing and play the *blues*. During his lifetime, he performed on street corners and in bars. He was famous for his ability to play such a wide variety of styles, from jazz to the pop music of his day, but today he is most famous for his unique interpretation of the blues.

Robert Johnson died in 1938, when he was only twenty-seven. He had recorded twenty-nine songs in the last years of his life, and these became enduring blues *classics*, including "Walking Blues" and "Sweet Home Chicago." His music expressed the hardships of being black in the South during the years of the Great Depression in such a powerful new way that listeners continue to identify with it—and it influenced the musicians that came later in the twentieth century, including B.B. King, Bob Dylan, and Eric Clapton. In 1961, an album of Robert Johnson's work, King of the Delta Blues Singers, was released, and in 1986, he was inducted into the Rock and Roll Hall of Fame as one of the musicians who shaped the beginnings of rock'n'roll.

Miles Davis

Miles Davis is another American musician who helped to shape the music of the twentieth century. He was born in 1926 in St. Louis; his father was a dentist, and his mother a music teacher. In 1941 he began playing the trumpet with St. Louis jazz bands, and he would eventually be considered one of the greatest jazz bandleaders and composers. He also led new movements in jazz, including bebop and jazz fusion.

Miles Davis died in 1992, but his music and influence continues as strong as ever. Rolling Stone magazine identified him as the musician with the deepest influence on rock music of all musicians. His 1959 album *Kind of Blue* has sold more than four million copies, and he was inducted into the Rock and Roll Hall of Fame in 2006.

Elvis Presley

Elvis Presley was born in 1935 in a two-room house in Mississippi. He and his parents moved to Memphis, Tennessee, in 1948, where Elvis soaked up the pop and country music of the time, as well as the gospel music he heard in church and the black **R&B** he heard on the streets.

In 1954, Elvis began his singing and recording career. Only two years later, he had become an international sensation who both shocked and excited the world. He created a new sound and style that blurred the lines between "white" and "black" music, and he began a whole new era of American music and popular culture. According to Rolling Stone magazine, "it was Elvis who made rock'n'roll the international language of pop." Rolling Stone also said that Elvis Presley was "an American music giant of the twentieth century who single-handedly changed the course of music and culture in the mid-1950s."

Elvis was more than just a musician. His recordings, dance moves, attitude, and clothing created a new culture in America. For the first time, young people had their own music, a sound and style all their own that would shape the decades to come. He died in 1977, but he will never be forgotten.

Grandmaster Flash

The boy who would become Grandmaster Flash was born as Joseph Saddler in 1958 in Barbados, an island in the Caribbean Sea. As a child, he and his family moved to New York City. His father had a huge

Today's hip-hop artists, including Drake, have Grandmaster Flash to thank for helping to shape a new genre of music.

record collection, which fascinated Joseph as he was growing up. After high school, he became a DJ and took the name Grandmaster Flash.

Like Elvis Presley, Flash helped to usher in a new era of sound and culture. He and his group, the Furious Five, created a form of music that

Research Project

This chapter tells the story of a few musicians. Pick another well-known musician and find out more about him or her. Use the library and the Internet to answer these questions: Where and when was this musician born? What shaped the early life of this musician? How did his or her musical career begin? What is this person most famous for today? What did you learn from this person's life?

was made by voices rapping combined with a DJ manipulating records in new ways. He helped start hip-hop music, using break-beats—remixing and creating new music using vinyl records and turntables as if they were musical instruments. According to Rolling Stone, Flash proved that rap was the voice of the inner city. He helped give the entire world a new way to express themselves through music.

Madonna

Women have always made music, just like men have, but for many centuries, women had much fewer opportunities to be professional musicians. That began to change in the twentieth century, and Madonna Louise Ciccone was one of the talented musicians who proved just what a woman could do. Born in 1958 in Michigan, she was one of six children. Her mother died when Madonna was six, leaving her father, an engineer at Chrysler, to raise his children alone. Madonna began studying dance when she was fourteen, and started writing her own songs when she was twenty-three. She performed her songs in New York City

Text-Dependent Questions

1. Explain what "pitch" is.
2. Define rhythm. What are some examples of rhythm outside music?
3. What is melody?
4. How are harmony and melody related?
5. What do composers do?

clubs, and eventually, she attracted the attention of record companies.

Like Elvis Presley, Madonna shocked people—and like Elvis, she also became a cultural *icon*. She was a superstar throughout the 1980s and 1990s, but she continues to constantly reinvent both her music and herself. She has sold more than 300 million records worldwide and is recognized as the best-selling female recording artist of all time.

CHANGES IN THE MUSIC WORLD

These famous musicians are a very small sampling of the world's best musicians. But not all of the great musicians throughout history became famous. Europe was the birthplace of what is today known as classical music, and these are the ones we know the most about—but meanwhile, musicians on the world's other continents were also forming their own kinds of music. In today's global world, those sounds blend together and influence each other. They are creating yet another era in music's long, long history.

Words to Understand

philosophers: People who study and deeply think about the nature of thoughts, reality, and existence.

ballads: Songs that tell a story in short verses.

lyrics: The words of a piece of music.

technology: Something that humans invent to make a job easier or to do something new.

synthesizers: Digital devices that generate artifical musical sounds.

media: Ways of communicating with many people at once, such as television or newspapers.

Chapter Two

The History
of Music

Music is a very ancient form of art. It may, in fact, be just about as old as human beings are. It has gone through many stages from prehistoric to modern.

ANCIENT MUSIC

Prehistoric people did not write down their music, so we can't know what it sounded like. However, we know that it existed because archeologists have found old, old musical instruments. A flute made from a bear's leg bone found in Slovenia is thought to be at least 40,000 years old. Other ancient flutes and stringed instruments have been found in India and China.

An Egyptian painting from nearly 4,000 years ago shows three musicians.

ASIAN MUSIC

India's classical music is one of the oldest musical traditions in the world. Sculptures from five thousand years ago show that dance and various musical instruments were part of the culture, and this ancient form of music is still performed today. It is monophonic, which means it has melody without harmony, with a very simple texture.

China also had its own ancient music, which lasted about three thousand years and shaped the musical styles of the surrounding regions. Chinese *philosophers*, including Confucius, believed that music was an important part of living in harmony with the universe. "Correct" music

Chinese musicians perform using ancient traditional instruments.

was thought to have instruments that corresponded to the elements of nature, and it helped create moral citizens and wise governments. China developed its own instruments, and its music was based on melody rather than harmony.

EUROPEAN MUSIC

The foundations of European music were laid in Ancient Greece, where music was an important part of social and cultural life. Greek theater was a popular art form, and music was essential to these performances. Choruses made up of both men and women also performed for

A painting on an ancient piece of Greek pottery from nearly 3,000 years ago shows a music teacher with his students.

entertainment, celebration, and spiritual ceremonies. Boys (but not girls!) were taught music starting when they were six years old, since music was considered necessary to being a well-rounded human being. The Greeks developed a music theory that eventually became the basis for Europe's religious and classical music.

During the Middle Ages in Europe, religious chanting was one of the most important forms of music, influenced by both the Ancient Greeks and the music of the Jewish synagogue. It was a monophonic, vocal form of music, usually sung by monks and nuns. In the Middle Ages, music wasn't only something used to worship God, however. Non-religious music also thrived as a form of entertainment in royal courts and

A stringed instrument called a lute was popular during the Middle Ages. This thirteenth-century painting shows a Muslim musician performing with a Christian musician for Portugal's King Alfonso X.

ordinary communities. Traveling musicians spread these dances songs, **ballads**, and love songs throughout Europe. Their **lyrics** often included clever rhymes.

People began to develop better ways to write down music in the Middle Ages, and with the invention of the printing press in the fifteenth century, music could more easily be spread across regions. Professional musicians worked for the church, royal courts, and towns. Composers of new music became increasingly important.

In the seventeenth century, music became more complex. It was performed by orchestras, large groups of musicians playing many instruments. Composers more and more created music not only for the church

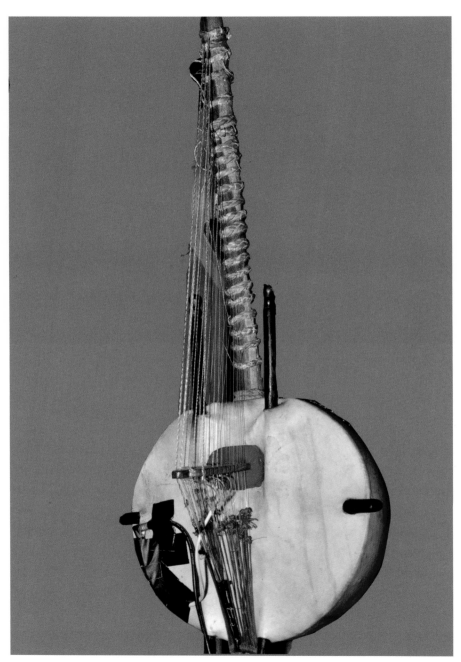

This twelve-stringed instrument from West Africa, called a kora, was an early version of the banjo.

but also for a new form of artistic entertainment—the opera, a type of theater where singers and musicians performed together to tell a story. Music now had rich harmonies, with many voices and instruments weaving together.

Public concerts became a popular form of entertainment during the eighteenth century. Orchestras were still popular, but the popular music of the day tended to be more singable, with a simpler, recognizable melody.

By the nineteenth century, music had become much less rigid in its forms. Passionate, emotional music became popular. Instead of following strict musical rules, musicians tried to develop their own unique ways of expressing themselves. This was called the Romantic Period of music.

Then, with the dawn of the twentieth century, music changed completely. With the invention of the radio and the phonograph, more and more people turned to music as a form of entertainment. Musicians explored new rhythms, styles, and sounds.

AFRICAN MUSIC

While other styles of music were developing in Asia and Europe, an ancient and rich style of music was growing in the vast continent of Africa. North Africa's music was more influenced by the music of Ancient Greece and the Near East. The music in sub-Saharan Africa had its own unique flavor in each region, but all of it depended heavily on rhythm. Music was not so much something that was performed for an audience, as it was something in which entire communities participated. There were work songs, with rhythms that helped a day's labor go more easily. There were also songs that went along with childbirth, marriage, and death. Music also helped shape people's connection to the spiritual world.

Like other regions of the world, Africa developed its own versions of

Louis Armstrong was one of the great musicians of the Jazz Era. Like all jazz musicians, Armstrong could improvise skillfully. Improvisation—creating spontaneous in-the-moment musical compositions—is an important part of jazz. Armstrong was also one of the first musicians to use "scat," a form of wordless, vocal improvisation.

flutes and string instruments, but percussion instruments were especially important in Africa. These included all kinds of drums, rattles, and shakers. In contrast to Europe, where polyphony—many melodies harmonizing together—developed and became popular, Africa developed polyrhythms, complicated patterns of simultaneous beats.

When the people of Africa were stolen and carried to the Americas as slaves, they brought with them their rich musical heritage. Their music would eventually create entire new musical genres in America.

AMERICAN MUSIC

Without the influence of African music, American music would never have been the same. Africa's strong rhythms helped shape the blues, jazz, and rock'n'roll.

Both jazz and rock music emerged from the blues, a form of music that came out of African American communities in the Deep South. The blues expressed the sadness of being black in the American South, but it also turned that sadness into something beautiful that all people could relate to. The blues continued as an important form of music, even as other music genres grew from it.

Jazz was born and became an important genre of music during the first half of the twentieth century. It started in African American communities in the Southern United States, but it didn't stay there. Soon white people loved this new music as much as black people did, and it spread from America around the world. As it did so, new distinctive styles of jazz were born: swing, bebop, ragtime, Dixieland, ska jazz, soul jazz, punk jazz, and jazz fusion are just a few. In 1988, a jazz musician named J. J. Johnson said, "Jazz is restless. It won't stay put and it never will."

In the second half of the twentieth century, rock music became yet another popular form of music, based on the blues and country music. The sound of rock often centers on a guitar. In rock music's most classic form, it has three chords, a strong back beat, and a catchy melody. An

Hip-hop is an entire culture that includes fashion, dance, and visual art expressions, as well as music. These breakdancers from Thailand show the way hip-hip has traveled around the world.

Research Project

This chapter mentions several new inventions that changed the music world, starting with the printing press and ending with the Internet. Some of these new inventions changed how music spread around the world, while others changed the way music was produced. Use the library or the Internet to find out more about how new technology has had an impact on music. List at least ten inventions that have changed the music world and describe how and why they did so.

electric bass guitar, drums, and keyboard instruments usually lay down the backbeat, though with the creation of new electronic *technology*, *synthesizers* and other digital instruments became popular too. Like jazz, rock branched out into different subgenres that ranged from blues rock and jazz-rock fusion to heavy metal and punk rock.

MUSIC TODAY

In the twentieth century, television began to play an increasingly important role in spreading music and making new music popular. Meanwhile, the development of new recording technology gave sound engineers an increasingly important role in popular music. By using recording techniques, sound engineers could create new sounds and sound effects that were not possible using traditional "live" music techniques.

Starting in the 1970s, music turned into a big business. Five enormous

Today, many people watch music videos on the Internet to find new artists and songs. The Internet has changed the way people listen to music and sell it.

record companies controlled the industry. (They later turned into four, with two of them joining together.) In the 1990s, a new trend in the music industry began, with music companies merging with film, television, and other **media** companies. This meant that record companies could promote musicians in many ways.

New technology also meant new sounds. It helped give birth to hip-hop's rap music. In 1990, a writer for *Time* magazine wrote, "Rap is

Text-Dependent Questions

1. Describe ancient Chinese music.
2. Discuss how European music changed over the course of centuries.
3. What was the strongest element of African music?
4. Explain the quotation, "Jazz is restless."
5. What are some genres of music that began in America?
6. How does hip-hop music compare to rock'n'roll?

the rock'n'roll of the day. Rock'n'roll was about attitude, rebellion, a big beat, sex and, sometimes, social comment. If that's what you're looking for now, you're going to find it here"—in rap. It's a genre that continued to grow into the twenty-first century, as it also spread around the world.

New technology meant other new things for the music industry. Throughout most of the twentieth century, the only way you could make much money as a musician was to get a record company to produce and sell your music. Today, though, thanks to both the Internet and new recording technology, musicians have many new opportunities. They don't necessarily need the big companies anymore to get their music out to the world. And some of them have become very successful in the music business world!

Words to Understand

open mics: Events where anyone can sign up to perform without getting paid.

rights: Legal ownership of a piece of art. If you own the rights, you can sell it and make money.

promoting: Getting the word out; publicizing.

marketing: Advertising or generally convincing people to buy a product.

distribute: Get products out to the places where people will buy them.

Chapter Three

The Business
of Music

For professional musicians, their work is more than just a fun way to express themselves—it's also a business. Many musicians will be happy making music in their free time and performing for friends and at *open mics*—but musicians who want to spend their lives making music will need to earn enough money to support themselves.

The music industry has changed dramatically since the beginning of digital music sales. Since 2000, recorded music sales have gone down significantly, while playing music live has become more important for artists looking to make money from their music. Today, music fans buy music online instead of in a store. Apple's iTunes is the largest music retailer in the world. Independent labels—music companies who

A musician may use a recording studio to turn her live music into a form of physical media that can be bought and sold.

aren't one of the enormous major music companies—have growing success. Even though the way that music is distributed and sold has changed, however, there are still a few main ways to make money as a musician.

COMPOSITIONS

One way to make money in the music business is by being a songwriter or a composer. Once you create a piece of music, you have a couple of choices (if it's good enough that other people what to perform it too). You can sell the **rights** to that song to someone else, such as a recording company or another musician. You'll get paid a one-time amount of money, and then the song will belong to whoever bought it from you. Another way to earn money from your song would be to sign a publishing contract. The publishing company then collects money whenever that piece of music is used or performed. As the songwriter or composer, you would get royalties—a small percentage of the money collected. Sheet music creates an income stream this way that can last forever.

RECORDINGS

Recordings are created by recording artists. Recordings were once made in recording studios, which were paid a daily or hourly rate for a recording session. Advances in recording technology, however, have allowed many producers and artists to create their own home studios, so that they no longer need recording studios.

In the old days, record companies almost always owned recording. A recording contract spelled out the business relationship between a recording artist and the record company. In a traditional contract, the company provided an advance to the musician (an amount of money he got as soon as he signed the contract). The musician agreed to record music that would be owned by the company, and after that, the musician

New inventions not only change the way we listen to music, but also the way it is sold.

Make Connections: Other Jobs in Music

 A record producer oversees all aspects of the recording, making many of the financial and artistic decisions in cooperation with the artist. Audio engineers (including recording, mixing, and mastering engineers) are responsible for the audio quality of the recording. A recording session may also require the services of an arranger or studio musicians. These jobs may not be as important, though, as more musicians use home studios.

would get a portion of the income from the recording. The company paid for the recording costs and the cost of *promoting* and *marketing* the record. The company also paid to manufacture and *distribute* the physical recordings (vinyl records or CDs, for example). Today, these arrangements still exist with big record companies, but as more and more musicians choose other options for their music, smaller record companies (known as "indies") will form business relationships with both musicians and other companies to handle many of these tasks.

Session musicians and orchestra members (as well as a few recording artists in special markets) are under contract to provide work-for-hire. This means they usually only get paid one-time fees or regular wages for their services, rather than a percentage of sales.

MEDIA

So far we've talked about the creative side of the music business, but in the modern world, the physical media (such as CDs) are sold as a

Becoming a music teacher who instructs children is one way for musicians to earn a living. Teachers at public schools need to go to college, where they'll take both education classes and music classes.

Make Connections: When Music Is Broadcast

When you hear music on the radio, the composers and recording artists get still another kind of payment, which is usually smaller than what they get from media. Muzak—the music you might hear while standing in an elevator, for example—makes the same kind of payments. Television shows and films that use music have yet another kind of payment system. If your song was picked for a television commercial or a movie, you could end up making a lot of money all at once. Subscription services (such as Rhapsody) can also provide an income stream to record companies and musicians.

product to people who want to take it home and own it. Music retailers sell the CDs, while a music distributor delivers the media from the manufacturer to the retailer. The music retailer pays the distributor, who in turn pays the record company for the recordings. The record company pays a certain amount of money to the publisher and composer or songwriter, as well as to the recording artist.

Today, music doesn't have to be bought recorded on a physical object of some kind; instead, it can be downloaded onto the buyer's computer, MP3 player, or some other electronic device. In the case of these digital downloads, or streams, there's no physical media other than the buyer's hard drive. Large online shops—such as Amazon—may pay the labels directly, while other digital distributors can also still be part of the chain between the music producer and the music buyer.

Make Connections: More Jobs in Music

Successful musicians usually have a road crew, workers who travel with the musicians on tour. A tour manager heads up this group of workers who provide stage lighting, live sound reinforcement, musical instrument tuning and maintenance, and transportation. On large tours, the road crew might also include an accountant, a stage manager, and a catering staff to make sure everyone has regular meals to eat. Local crews from the area around each venue are often hired to help move equipment on and off stage. On small tours, though, a few "roadies"—or the musicians themselves—might handle all these jobs.

LIVE MUSIC

The oldest kind of musical performance is live music. Even in today's world of CDs and streaming, live performance is still an important side of the music business. A promoter or booking agency usually brings together performing artists with venue owners to arrange contracts and book performances. Then you and your friends can buy the tickets either from the venue or from a ticket distribution service such as Ticketmaster. The musicians and their managers decide when and where to give live performances. Record companies may provide the money for musicians to go on tour, giving live performances around the country or the world.

Make Connections: Still More Jobs in Music

Very successful musicians have a lot of details to worry about. They may hire people from other fields to help them out, so that they have more time to focus on their music. A manager oversees all aspects of musicians career in exchange for a percentage of the income. An entertainment lawyer helps musicians with the details of contracts and other deals. A business manager handles payments, taxes, and bookkeeping.

NEW WAYS OF DOING BUSINESS

The music business has changed a lot in the twenty-first century, and it will probably continue to change. The definite lines that once divided musicians, publishers, record companies, distributors, retail (store owners), and the buyers have started to get blurry. There are lots of new possibilities today. Some musicians own their own publishing companies. Management companies sometimes promote and market recordings on behalf of their clients, and some electronics companies have become digital music retailers. Most important of all, individual musicians today have new opportunities to promote and market themselves using YouTube or other forms of social media. It's a whole new world!

MAKING MONEY AS A MUSICIAN

That doesn't mean it's easy to get rich as a musician. It still takes a lot of hard work and talent.

Research Project

Go online to the Bureau of Labor and Statistics' Occupational Outlook Handbook (http://www.bls.gov/ooh/entertainment-and-sports/home.htm) to find out more about what you might expect from a career in music. Describe the personal qualities the BLS says musicians need. What does it say about training and advancement? According to the BLS, what are some of the difficulties that go along with being a musician? Tell your class what you discover.

The U.S. Bureau of Labor Statistics (BLS) provides some information on what sorts of jobs musicians can expect, and how much money they can expect to make. In 2012, the BLS reported that musicians made on average $23.50 hour. That means that a musician who worked full time, forty hours a week, fifty-two weeks a year, would make close to $50,000 a year. However, being a musician isn't a nine-to-five sort of job. You might only work on weekends, for example, or whenever you can get a gig. Some weeks you might not work at all. According to the BLS, music directors, composers, and songwriters have about the same earnings and opportunities. Keep in mind that the numbers reported by the BLS are just the average; some people made a lot more and some made a lot less. Between now and 2022, the BLS predicts that opportunities for musicians will grow very slowly.

Musicians are often able to make more money if they're willing to work part or full time at another job. Those other jobs could be totally

Text-Dependent Questions

1. Describe some of the ways the music business has changed recently. Why have these changes come about?
2. What are two ways to sell musical compositions?
3. List some of the jobs that are centered on recording music.
4. How are session musicians paid? How is this different from the payment other recording musicians receive?
5. How have YouTube and other social media sites changed the music business?

unrelated to music, or they could have a lot to do with music. For example, a musician might dedicate twenty hours a week to music, and work another twenty or thirty hours in a restaurant, store, or some other business. Some musicians might work full time as teachers, and use their weekends and summers for performances.

There are lots of possibilities out there—and some of them might be great opportunities for you to get involved in the music business!

Words to Understand

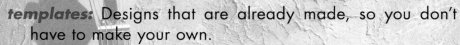

templates: Designs that are already made, so you don't have to make your own.

customize: Change to suit your needs or desires.

press kit: A collections of photos, articles, or other materials that you use to promote yourself.

collaborate: Work together on a project.

Chapter Four

How Can I Get Involved in Music?

If want a career in music, the most important first step is to become as good at music as you possibly can. Whether that's playing an instrument, singing, or composing music, you'll need to learn and practice as much as you possibly can.

CLASSES AND TRAINING

Some musicians are self-taught, but most have taken at least some sort of classes. You might find a guitar or piano instructor, for example, who will teach you one-on-one. School and community orchestras, bands, and choirs are another way for you to learn and get practice performing. Getting a college degree in music isn't all that important for performers. (It is important, though, if you want to do something else connected to

Becoming a musician takes hours and hours of practice.

music, such as teach music in a school or college.) Going to college and getting a degree in music doesn't mean you'll automatically become a successful musician—but they are good places to learn from your professors and fellow students. You'll have new opportunities to perform at college, too, and you might meet people who can help you start your career. What's most important for performers is being really, really good—and then letting the world know!

PRACTICE

The best musicians didn't start out that way. They have been practicing for years and years. No matter what level of musician you are now, practice will make you better.

You should also take every opportunity you can to perform in front of an audience, even if you're not getting paid. The more you perform, the more comfortable you'll feel on stage. You'll get used to it and feel less nervous. And who knows? Someone in the audience might like you so much that it will lead to a paying gig.

OTHER STEPS TOWARD A CAREER IN MUSIC

Make a Plan

Making a great plan is important for pretty much anything you do in life. It's like your roadmap for the future. You can adjust it as you go along, but it will keep you focused, working toward specific goals. Once you've accomplished one, your plan will tell you what your next step will be. It will give you direction.

Try to make your goals as specific as possible. Instead of saying, "I want to be rich and famous," you might want to say, "I want to have at least one paying gig a month by the end of this year." Then break down your big goals into smaller tasks—for example, "find a list of local venues," and "contact five new venues this week." This will make your plan more manageable. Instead of getting overwhelmed and discouraged by how far you have to go, you'll feel encouraged as you achieve your smaller goals.

Manage Your Time Wisely

Say you want to be one of today's indie musicians, selling your music directly online without worrying about a recording company or even a manager. That sounds great, but it's not as easy as it might sound. Independent musicians have to wear many hats; they have to handle the practical business tasks, as well as the more creative parts of being a musician. It can be easy to end up so focused on marketing and

Being part of a school ensemble is a good way to learn important skills if you think you want to become a professional musician.

scheduling that you lose track of why you became a musician in the first place—because you love to make music!

Learning how to manage your time now will help you as you build a music career. Right now you might be juggling schoolwork, an after-school job, your household chores, practice, and some music gigs, while later on in life, you'll have other responsibilities to manage—but you can develop time-management tasks now that will help you later in life.

Figure out your priorities. Set aside definite times for each thing that's important to you and make sure that something that's not as impor-tant isn't taking up too much of your time. For example, you may think that watching music videos helps inspire you as a musician—but if you notice that you're spending hours watching videos and very little time practicing, you probably have a problem. Create a realistic schedule that has time slots for each thing you need to do.

If there's anything you are doing that's not bringing you closer to your goals, stop and think. If you're spending hours each day on tasks that aren't helping you reach your goals, see what you can do to get rid of them, simplify them, or postpone them. Maybe you could give some of the jobs to someone else (for example, you could hire your little brother to hang up posters for you), so that you can focus on what is truly most important for your career.

Build a Team

Even if you're a soloist, a team of people working with you can help you build a music career. And if you're in a band, working together can be a big help. Each of you will have unique skills to bring to the team, and you can help each other stay excited and enthused. Bouncing ideas off each other and planning together can keep you moving forward.

Make a Website

In today's world, all businesses need websites, and musicians especially need them. The Internet is a great way to advertise and sell your music. Your website should show people who you are and what your music sounds like.

Setting up a website isn't very hard, especially with all the tools available today. You don't have to know computer code or any special skills in order to create a website. You can use ready-made **templates** to launch your own websites, such as WordPress. These sites allow you to **customize** your own site from the templates, add the information you need, and upload examples of your work.

A website allows people to contact you as well. If someone sees your work and thinks you'd be perfect for an event he's setting up at a local venue, he can send you an e-mail. Without a website, it's a lot harder

Forming a band can be a good way to grow as a young musician.

for people to get in touch with you. And it's harder for you to show people what you and your music are like.

Then tell people you have a website! Tell all your friends to tell their friends. Send out an e-mail to everyone you know. Hang posters around town or school with your website's information on them. Use Facebook or Twitter to tell the world about your new website. As word gets around, hopefully more and more people will see your site. They'll have the chance to hear your music and get excited about it.

Use the Internet in Other Ways Too

The Internet is full of ways to let people know about you and your music. Besides the big social media sites, here are a few other sites you might want to check out:

- AmieStreet.com: A social network and music marketplace from Amazon for indie artists. The site gives the artists 70 percent of the sale.
- Artistopia.com: An online venue where performers can post a profile and display their work.
- BandBuzz.com: A social network where artists can set up a profile, upload their music, and get reviewed and recommended by users.
- Elisteningpost.com: A way for musicians to upload their music and sell it just about anywhere they want.
- Popfolio.net: A music widget provider for blogs that lets independent musicians upload their songs for possible sales.
- PumpAudio.com: A service intended to help indie artists get their music licensed for television and film.
- Sonicbids.com: Allows you to construct a low-cost electronic **press kit** that can be constantly updated so the latest version is always available.
- Unsigned.com: A site for unsigned bands to put up a profile page and host a playlist of MP3s to attract new listeners.

Research Project

Use the Internet to find the websites of local musicians. What are things you notice about their sites? What does each site tell you? What details from each site would you want to imitate if you were creating your own website? What would you want to do differently?

Network

Networking is just talking to everyone you know—and everyone they know—about your music. Get in the habit of letting people know that you're a musician. This doesn't mean being obnoxious and pushy—but it doesn't mean being shy either! Be friendly. Listen as well as talk. If people like you, they'll be more likely to be interested in your music too.

One good way to network is to **collaborate** with another musician by sharing a gig. That way you'll have a chance to add her fans to yours—and vice versa. And don't expect people to help you out without being willing to help them out too!

After a gig, hang out and talk to the people who attended. Doing free gigs can be a good way to network too. Even if you don't get paid, every gig is an opportunity to connect with other people in ways that may lead to new opportunities.

Build a Niche

A "niche" is your personal little corner of the music world. It might be built around your particular genre of music and your unique style as a musician, but it could also be built around your personal beliefs. Maybe

Text-Dependent Questions

1. Using the samples given in the text, make your own example of specific, short-term goal.
2. Why is time management important for musicians?
3. List three ways you could tell people about your website.
4. What does networking involve?
5. Explain what a "niche" is, according to this chapter.

you want to create a new kind of Christian music. Or maybe you want to use your music to speak out on environmental issues. Having a niche will help you connect with the people who are more likely to become your fans. Start small and local, focusing on the people living in your community who share your interests—and build out gradually from there to other cities and regions. As you grow, don't leave your niche behind. Stay true to what really excites you.

GET STARTED NOW!

Building a career as a musician isn't easy. Very few musicians have overnight success. So if you're considering music as a career path, begin right now. Practice every chance you get. Talk to any musicians you run into and pick their brains. How did they get where they are today? What steps did they take first? Do they have any advice for you? Read books about musicians. Research various musical careers, besides being a performer. Learn what your options are. Then you'll be ready for whatever the future holds!

Find Out More

Online

Biz Kids Guide to Writing a Business Plan
bizkids.com/wp/wp-content/uploads/Kids-Business-Plan.pdf

Careers in Music
www.careersinmusic.com

Music Careers
www.music-careers.com

Music Industry Careers
musicians.about.com

In Books

Klickstein, Gerald. *The Musician's Way: A Guide to Practice, Performance, and Wellness.* New York: Oxford University Press, 2009.

Michael, Ted. *So You Wanna Be a Superstar? The Ultimate Audition Guide.* Philadelphia, PA: Running Press, 2012.

Murphy, M.J. *Choosing Notes: Creativity, Ear Training, Harmony, & Music Theory.* Seattle, OR: Twilight Storm Media, 2013.

Rankin, Kenrya. *Start It Up: The Complete Teen Business Guide to Turning Your Passions into Pay.* San Francisco, CA: Zest Books, 2011.

Reeves, Diane Lindsey. *Career Ideas for Kids Who Like Music and Dance.* New York: Checkermark, 2007.

Series Glossary of Key Terms

Abstract: Made up of shapes that are symbolic. You might not be able to tell what a piece of abstract art is just by looking at it.

Classical: A certain kind of art traditional to the ancient Greek and Roman civilizations. In music, it refers to music in a European tradition that includes opera and symphony and that is generally considered more serious than other kinds of music.

Culture: All the arts, social meanings, thoughts, and behaviors that are common in a certain country or group.

Gallery: A room or a building that displays art.

Genre: A category of art, all with similar characteristics or styles.

Impressionism: A style of painting that focuses more on the artist's perception of movement and lighting than what something actually looks like.

Improvisation: Created without planning or preparation.

Medium (media): The materials or techniques used to create a work of art. Oil paints are a medium. So is digital photography.

Pitch: How high or low a musical note is; where it falls on a scale.

Portfolio: A collection of some of the art an artist has created, to show off her talents.

Realism: Art that tries to show something exactly as it appears in real life.

Renaissance: A period of rapid artistic and literary development during the 1500s–1700s, or the name of the artistic style from this period.

Studio: A place where an artist can work and create his art.

Style: A certain way of creating art specific to a person or time period.

Technique: A certain way of creating a piece of art.

Tempo: How fast a piece of music goes.

Venue: The location or facility where an event takes place.

Index

About the Author

Z.B. Hill is a an author and publicist living in Binghamton, New York. He has a special interest in education and how art can be used in the classroom.

Picture Credits

Dreamstime.com:
19: Sbukley
34: Sebastian Czapnik
36: Paul Hakimata
54: Roxana González

Fotolia.com:
6: bst2012
8: donatas1205
12: Sanjay Goswami
22: Tryfonov
38: sumnersgraphicsinc
40: CandyBox Images
42: jovanmandic
48: MIGUEL GARCIA SAAVED

50: bradleyhebdon
52: Pavel Losevsky

13: Jazz Enthusiast
14: Cornell University Library Image
16: Joe Mazzola
24: The Yorck Project
25: Peter Morgan
26: Bibi Saint-Poi
27: Cantigas de Santa Maria
28: Kannan Shanmugam Studio
30: Library of Congress
32: Sry85